BAD BACKS

Leila Henderson, who is trained in therapeutic massage, is a former health and fitness writer for *Good Housekeeping* magazine. In researching this book she has realised that, as a mother of two young children and a keen runner, she is a prime candidate for back problems.

BAD BACKS
A Self-Help Guide

LEILA HENDERSON

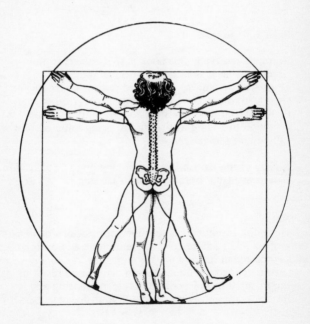

ROBINSON
London

Robinson Publishing Ltd
7 Kensington Church Court
London W8 4SP

First published in Great Britain by
Robinson Publishing Ltd 1995

ISBN 1–85487–388–1

Note
This book is not a substitute for your doctor's or health
professional's advice, and the publishers and author
cannot accept liability for any injury or loss to any
person acting or refraining from action as a result of
the material in this book. Before commencing any
health treatment, always consult your doctor.

Printed and bound in Great Britain

Contents

Introduction

After headaches and colds, back pain is the most common cause of lost work days. Four out of five of us will seek treatment for backache at some point in our lives. Why is back pain so widespread? One reason is natural wear and tear on the ageing human skeleton. Poor posture is another. Lack of fitness, unsafe working conditions and being overweight also play their part.

Ageing, itself, is not a leading factor; the most common age for back problems is between 25 and 50 years, although some forms of backache target the very young, others the elderly. It can affect anyone – manual labourers and the office bound, home workers and athletes.

The trigger which brings on severe pain can be a fall at work, trauma in a car accident, or a sudden, awkward movement. Whatever its cause, back pain is a surefire way to stop you enjoying life. No one but a fellow sufferer can understand your misery, though pretty well everyone will have an opinion and a pet cure.

This book sets out simple steps to self-management and sorts out some of the myths and facts about back pain. Here you will find out the physiotherapist's role, which sports are good for your back and which are not, and dozens of small changes you can make in your daily routine – the way you stand, sit and move – to relieve pain and prevent another attack.

Luckily, most back pain can be prevented or cured. Surgery is rare – and a last resort. Remember, though, that occasional niggles can become major problems if left untreated. Persistent back pain should always be investigated by a medical professional, starting with your family doctor. Early treatment is your best chance of making a permanent recovery.

Chapter 1
Ouch!
What Causes Back Pain?

Back pain is as individual as you are, and there are hundreds of possible causes. Over the years, the spine has to twist, bend, support and help lift heavy loads. It is prone to trauma through accidents, poor posture, physical stress and injuries to the discs, joints and ligaments. On top of that, there are degenerative problems associated with ageing and a variety of diseases which can trigger an aching back.

THE HEALTHY BACK

Your backbone is your body's chief means of support. It's a complex structure, made up of bones, known as vertebrae, separated by shock-absorbing discs. Ligaments and muscles ('soft tissues') bind the vertebrae together and strengthen the discs and joints – the hinges formed by the vertebrae. As well as holding you upright, the spine protects the delicate spinal cord from damage.

Strong, yet flexible, the 24 small bones of the movable spine are divided, for medical purposes, into three sections – neck (cervical), chest (thoracic) and lower back (lumbar). This does not take into account the five fused vertebrae of the pelvic (sacral) region, ending with the tail bone, or coccyx.

The healthy spine is 'S' shaped, with a slight curve at the neck and just above the hips.

WHERE'S THE PAIN?

Pain is the body's warning system. It's a sign that something's not functioning properly. And it can be deceptive; with back troubles, for instance, not all pain is felt in the back. Sometimes, it occurs in the groin, leg, foot, stomach wall or even the heel. Wherever it does happen, you may feel anything from a nagging ache to stabbing agony, or experience pins and needles, a burning sensation or numbness. Pain is often felt in the centre of the back, at or near the belt line.

Long-term back problems in the low back (the lumbar region) are more common than in any other part of the spine, but it's rare for any back disorder to occur in isolation. Pain, in any part of the spine, can be reflected upwards or downwards.

The bones of the spine

STRESSES AND STRAINS

The muscles, ligaments and joints can be injured in a fall or accident, by a sudden movement, long-term stress or poor posture and weak muscles. Most back injuries are not caused by damage to a bone but to the soft tissues (ligaments and muscles) surrounding the joint.

Sudden movement or unusual stress can tear muscle fibres or painfully overstretch the ligaments, which are the retaining walls for the soft discs that act as shock absorbers between the vertebrae. Chronic, long-term pain is rarely caused by strained muscles, which generally heal within a couple of weeks.

As the body ages, degenerative changes take place in the spine, but injury or stress can speed the process.

DISC DISORDERS

'Intervertebral' discs provide a flexible cushion between each bone in the spinal column. They help transmit loads, and can flatten, bend and twist. It's when one of these cushions goes wrong that horrible pain can occur.

Normal wear and tear combined with a sudden trauma can rupture the disc, causing the jelly-like fluid inside to bulge outwards or even through a damaged outer ligament. This is what is meant by the expression 'slipped disc'. The disc, in effect, loses its ability to absorb shock.

Sudden, sharp pain may immobilise you, but the lead-up to it – disc protrusion – happens gradually. The expression 'put my back out' is misleading; the discs are firmly anchored to the vertebrae above and below.

How do you know you have a bulging disc? One symptom is tiredness and a dull ache, sometimes after exertion, which disappears when you have rested. A protruding disc can prevent the vertebrae from lining up properly as you carry on your daily activities. To prevent pain, you may be forced to hold your upper body off-centre.

If you experience sudden pain and are unable to straighten up or move your back properly, you may have a bulging disc. The problem can happen anywhere in the movable spine, from the neck to the lower back, and can vary from slight tearing and inflammation of the outer fibres to a full-blown herniation, where the central material escapes.

Discs contain no nerve fibre. As it is impossible to feel pain without damage to nerves, disc disorders, in themselves, are painless. Pain in other parts of the body, often dismissed as rheumatism, could be caused by a bulging disc pressing on a nerve. It may, for instance, press painfully on the sciatic nerve, causing numbness or pins and needles in the lower leg or foot.

Never hesitate to see your doctor about any persistent pain. You are much more likely to recover completely if a disc disorder is treated in the early stages.

SCAR TISSUE

Once the soft tissues containing nerve fibres are damaged, pain will be felt until the injury has completely healed. But that's not the end of the story. The scar tissue which results is less elastic than normal tissue and tends to shorten. Movement of these shortened tissues can produce pain. The answer is to restore flexibility with appropriate treatment, prescribed by your doctor or physiotherapist. Without this, you may be feeling pain from the scar tissue even years after the original injury has healed.

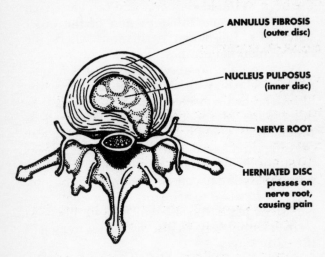

ANNULUS FIBROSIS
(outer disc)

NUCLEUS PULPOSUS
(inner disc)

NERVE ROOT

HERNIATED DISC
presses on
nerve root,
causing pain

Spinal column, top view

SCIATICA

The sciatic nerves run from the lower back, across the buttocks and down the backs of the legs. They can be irritated by a bulging disc or inflamed facet joint – a small spinal joint – but the pain can be felt anywhere along their paths. This is called referred pain. Referred pain from spinal disease can occur anywhere, in any limb.

Along with fibrositis, rheumatism and lumbago, sciatica is not classified as a disease. These are all words used by the general public to describe a wide range of symptoms.

ABNORMAL CURVATURE

Viewed from the side, the spine has three slight curves: one in the lower back, one in the upper back and one in the neck. From the back, the normal spine appears straight. Sometimes, however, there is a curve to one side. This curve is known as scoliosis. There are two major types:

1. Postural scoliosis, often caused by one leg being shorter than the other.

2. Structural scoliosis, due to diseases or abnormalities of the bones, muscles or nerves.

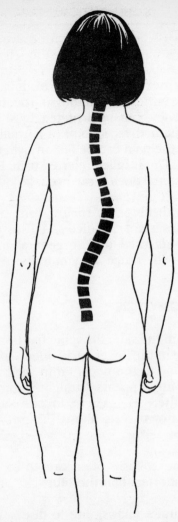

**Curvature to one side is called
Scoliosis**

A couple of decades ago, your dressmaker or tailor would have been the first to tell you that you had one leg shorter than the other. Now, few of us can afford our own dressmaker, so it's up to parents, teachers and community health workers to identify the problem in its early stages. This is not so difficult, if they know what to look for.

Parents should watch out for one, or all, of the following signs in their children – especially those between the ages of nine and 14, when the bones are growing rapidly:

1. One shoulder higher than the other.

2. One shoulder blade sticking out more than the other.

3. One arm longer than the other.

4. A bulge on either side of the back. Ask your child to bend forward, back parallel to the floor, arms relaxed and hanging down. Report any one-sided bulge to your doctor.

   With specific exercises, this problem can often be easily corrected or prevented from progressing.

Kyphosis is a less common form of abnormal curvature, causing the spine to bulge outwards, either in the lower back or chest area. Lordosis is an inward curve of the lower back. When the curve is excessive, it's known as 'swayback'.

ONE LEG SHORTER THAN THE OTHER

Because the difference is usually very slight, you may not realise you have one leg shorter than the other until your physiotherapist or doctor points it out. This very common condition can cause scoliosis, as described on page 7, and a variety of other problems, including hip rotation, which can create pain virtually anywhere in the spine. On the other hand, of the 80 per cent or so of the population who have one leg shorter than the other, many will never suffer any ill effects.

AGEING

You and your spine are getting older every day. It's only natural to expect a bit of wear and tear. But disc problems rarely crop up in the over-50s. The most likely age for disc disorders and low back pain is 30 to 50 years. Back pain in older people tends to be caused by stiffening joints and degenerative illness.

OTHER CONDITIONS

Injury and wear and tear are by far the most common causes of backache. However, your doctor will want to rule out the following:

Arthritis

All the joints can be affected by rheumatoid arthritis or the more common osteoarthritis. In the spine, this is often referred to as spondylosis. Symptoms include joint pain, swelling, redness or heat in a joint, stiffness or immobility.

Osteoporosis

Loss of calcium from the bones of the spine may result in partial collapse of the vertebrae, leading to postural problems and a high risk of bone fracture. This is most common in post-menopausal women. Diet and exercise are important preventive measures.

Osteomalacia

Like osteoporosis, this is a bone weakness caused by lack of calcium and sunlight or a failure to absorb nutrients.

Osteomyelitis

A bacterial infection of the spine which causes inflammation, osteomyelitis is usually accompanied by severe pain and fever. Your doctor will probably prescribe a suitable antibiotic.

Arachnoiditis

This painful condition occurs when the protective coverings surrounding the spinal cord and nerve roots become inflamed and thickened by scar tissue, due chiefly to a disorder of the spinal bones.

Ankylosing Spondylitis

This is a rare condition, more common in young men than women, in which the joints of the spine become inflamed and stiffen.

Tumours

Back tumours are rare and usually benign. Occasionally, however, a tumour may be a symptom of an illness such as cancer, leukaemia or Hodgkin's disease. Report any unusual lump or sensation of weakness or numbness to your doctor.

Emotional Stress

Tension can cause imbalances in the muscles and stir up existing problems. Back pain is often more evident when your emotional life is rocky.

Chapter 2
Backing Away from Occupational Hazards

Injuries to the vertebrae, discs, muscles and tendons are among the most common injuries in the workplace. Most are caused by over-exertion, rather than injury. In other words, most work-related back problems could be prevented by following safe practices, including maintaining good posture and using the right equipment.

The greatest number of back injuries are suffered by manual workers, machine operators and drivers, but no one is immune. You are at high risk if you do any of the following:

- Manual labour in which you lift heavy loads.
- Twist and bend frequently.
- Assembly-line work involving repetitive movements.
- Drive for long periods, especially in a vibrating vehicle, such as a truck or tractor.
- Sit or stand bending over for prolonged periods.
- Carry heavy, one-sided loads, as photographers do.

Housework often combines several of the above factors, so you are no less at risk if your workplace happens to be the home. Think of all the twisting and bending you do tidying, hanging clothes and making beds.

With a bit of effort and ingenuity, your body can work like a well-oiled machine all week long. Specialists in occupational health are now employed by most larger corporations to save countless work hours lost to back pain. Known as occupational physiotherapists or ergonomists, they train anyone, from long-distance lorry drivers to computer programmers and refuse men, on individual ways to improve posture and the work environment.

'Pause gymnastics' is proving a major factor in good back health. It means taking regular rest and exercise breaks to maintain correct posture (see 'Gently Does It', page 44). Even if you don't participate in a structured routine, a few minutes spent walking around can remobilise your joints and refresh your brain.

THE HOBBYIST

Is this you? You sit most of the day at work, put your feet up after dinner, then on weekends you throw yourself into your favourite pastime – hang-gliding, golf, gardening. Whatever the activity, the sudden change of pattern, from sedentary to active, can do irreparable damage to your back.

FACT FILE

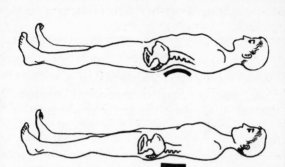

Pelvic Tilts – tilting the pelvis forward and back to mobilise the lower back – can be done while sitting, standing or lying down, as shown

Pelvic Tilts

A tip for anyone who sits for long periods – long-distance lorry drivers, taxi drivers, clerical workers and so on – is to get into the habit of doing 'pelvic tilts'. It only takes a few moments every half hour or so to tilt the pelvis forward and back to relieve pressure and to mobilise the lower back. Drivers can try practising this back-saver when they have stopped at traffic lights.

Back problems often happen after prolonged physical stress followed by a twisting movement which puts an unusual stress on the lower back. This is what is meant by putting your back out. Gardeners are prone to this type of injury, as they bend the back for long periods while digging or weeding.

FACT FILE

When you are in the middle of an attack of back pain, avoid anything which requires prolonged sitting, or excessive bending over and twisting – gardening, vacuuming, even picking up the baby.

Sometimes, the tiniest amount of bending can trigger an injury which has been developing for years – 'I just bent down to dust the stereo . . .' People who are generally unfit or who have poor posture are prime candidates for such sudden injury to the muscles, ligaments and discs. You can do a lot to avoid being the victim of immobilising back pain by practising the exercises and lifestyle changes listed in Chapters 5 and 6.

PARENTHOOD CAN BE PAINFUL

The joys of pregnancy can be marred when hormonal changes begin to soften the ligaments, in preparation for labour. It's all too easy to overstretch the joints of the pelvis and lower back, aggravating existing back troubles and creating new ones. This softening effect lasts for up to a year after the birth.

The other major change in pregnancy is weight increase and a shifting centre of gravity. Unless your stomach and back muscles are very strong, the weight of your uterus can pull you forward, exaggerating the curve of your lower back. For this reason, back pain is common during pregnancy. Often, however, discomfort occurs after the baby is born.

It's vital that newly pregnant women begin a programme of specific exercises to strengthen and stretch the back and tummy muscles. The routines in Chapter 5 are suitable for most pregnant women, but always check with your doctor before starting any exercise programme.

Nor are your troubles over when the baby finally arrives. You and your spouse will spend a substantial amount of time bending over your baby's cot or over a change table. That's not to mention the stooping and carrying which continues well into toddlerhood.

N.B. Remember that, in the second half of pregnancy, it's unwise to lie flat on your back for long periods. This can cause dizziness and restrict blood-flow to your heart.

Motherhood Checklist

- Do exercises to strengthen your back and stomach muscles.

- Attend a prenatal exercise class if there's one near you – ask your doctor or midwife.
- Avoid putting on too much weight.
- Rest on your side on a good bed, using a pillow to support your top leg.
- Most sports are fine while you're pregnant, as long as they don't allow your body to overheat. Some, such as skiing, horse-riding and cycling, may result in falls and should be avoided.
- When feeding, use a good back support – get advice from a community midwife or health visitor.
- Invest in a good, waist-height (or slightly higher) change table. Cots, too, should be at the right height, to minimise stooping.
- Kneel down if you occasionally have to change nappies on a bed or the floor.
- Tall women and men should use a buggy with adjustable handles, to avoid stooping as they push.

DANCING TO A STANDSTILL

Dancing can be great exercise for the back because it encourages loose, flexible joints. But professional dancing, especially ballet, can involve holding the body rigidly for many minutes at a time, thus straining the back.

Like many professional sportspeople, dancers may be storing up trouble for themselves. Thirty-four per cent of dancing injuries are spinal, with male dancers, who lift females high in the air, particularly at risk.

Dancers should:

- Warm up adequately, especially before a demanding rehearsal.
- Pace themselves in rehearsal.
- Warm up again after any break of more than half an hour.
- Create a strong 'centre' in the abdomen.
- Develop strength and balance.

Most large dance companies employ physiotherapists and other body-care specialists to try to minimise the stress put on their dancers' muscles, ligaments and joints. Adequate rest and stretching do help, but a lifetime of dancing inevitably leads to wear and tear on the spine.

Having said all that, tap-dancing happens to be a great aerobic exercise for those with unstable backs. In tap, the spine takes little stress, while the legs work like crazy.

Everyday Back Care

1 Always be aware of how you are using your back.

2 Unless you can sit with your feet flat on the ground, use a footrest. Whenever possible, stand with one foot supported on a footrest, knee bent.

3 Spend some time each day in a rocking chair – it rests the back by alternating the muscle groups used.

4 Keep your tummy flat. Pull in your abdominal muscles whenever you remember while sitting, standing, walking or exercising. The abdominals are the only front support muscles for your back.

5 Likewise, use your buttock muscles to keep your bottom tucked under.

6 Don't wear high heels which throw your weight forward.

7 Don't spend a lot of time sitting on soft chairs or deep sofas.

8 Shoulder bags are to blame for a lot of back pain. Try to even the balance of loads carried by wearing a backpack or carrying a bag of shopping in each hand.

9 Big-breasted women often complain of shoulder and neck pain. The answer is to wear a bra with wide shoulder straps. In extreme cases, a breast reduction can give relief.

10 Avoid spending a lot of time with your neck twisted to one side. For example, choose a cinema seat directly in front of the screen, not to one side.

Chapter 3
Back-Stop Medical Help

Back pain is a symptom, just as fever is a symptom. Determining the underlying cause is the work of your doctor and other health professionals such as physiotherapists and, sometimes, orthopaedic surgeons, neurologists or neurosurgeons. Having established the source of the pain, they can set about remedying it and possibly referring you to other specialists in the field.

It's not absolutely necessary to have a doctor's referral to make an appointment to see a physiotherapist, chiropractor or osteopath (although on the NHS it *is* necessary, if you wish to try and get free treatment), but if this is the first time you have had back pain or the condition has suddenly changed or got worse, you should certainly consult your doctor first.

QUESTIONS YOUR DOCTOR MAY ASK

Because of the network of nerves in and around the spine, it may be difficult for your doctor to identify the root of the problem. Any information you can give him or her will be useful. For example:

- When did the pain start?
- Was there a specific moment of onset or did the pain start gradually?
- What were you doing at the time?
- Have you a history of back pain?
- What makes the pain worse?
- What makes it better?

Your doctor will also ask you questions about your general health and happiness to give a broad idea of your lifestyle and its relevance to your current predicament.

OH, THE RELIEF!

On your first visit to your GP, you may not be receptive to suggestions of long-term self management of your back problem. Reasonably enough, most of us don't want to put up with pain any longer than necessary. We tend to look to our family doctor for fast relief when a couple of Panadols don't do the trick.

Depending on your pain level and condition, your doctor may suggest one of four groups of drugs. The properties and possible side effects of these drugs are detailed on page 81.

1. The first group is analgesics, or pain killers, starting with paracetamol and progressing to the stronger paracetamol-codeine combinations.

2. Second are the muscle relaxants, which help to relieve muscle spasms and allow cleansing blood to flow to the damaged area.

3. Third are non-steroidal anti-inflammatory drugs, which help to reduce the inflammation around a sore joint.

4. The fourth drug group, cortico-steroid injections, is somewhat controversial. It's used only in extreme cases, when neither bed rest nor pills has worked. A cortico-steroid can be injected directly into the spine. Or, where there are disc problems and compression of the nerves, it can be injected next to the nerves to ease local inflammation.

PAIN CLINICS

Rather than put chronic (long-term) pain sufferers on an extended course of pain-killing drugs, the doctor may suggest a pain clinic, usually based at a large hospital. At such clinics, patients may be asked to keep a logbook of their pain, noting when it occurs and giving it a rating, from zero (lowest) to 10 (most severe). Each case is discussed by a variety of health professionals, including a psychologist, occupational therapist, physiotherapist, anaesthetist, psychiatrist, rheumatologist and others. These specialists assess a patient's entire lifestyle and health picture, not just the back problem. Relaxation techniques and postural retraining are integral parts of the pain-management plan.

TAKING A CLOSER LOOK

Discovering the source of back pain is no easy matter. In some cases, your doctor may take blood tests and/or refer you for X-rays of the spine, to reveal any abnormality of the bone – one of the least common causes of backache – or poor alignment of the spine. Also, if the space between two vertebrae appears too narrow, it may indicate an old disc injury which is causing new pain: when one joint ceases to do its job, the other joints have to take the strain.

Problems in the soft tissues – the muscles, ligaments and discs – do not show up on ordinary X-rays. There's a variety of ways to identify a troublesome disc. Myelograms and discograms are variations on the X-ray technique. Both are unpleasant procedures involving spinal injections and are losing favour to CAT scan X-rays which, in effect, give a three-dimensional picture of the spine. Magnetic Resonance Imagery seems to be the most reliable diagnostic technique of all. It uses magnetic fields to make a three-dimensional image of bones and muscles.

SURGERY

Surgery for back problems is a last resort. By the time it becomes obvious that surgery is necessary, you will have been in a lot of pain for a long time. You will have read most of the magazines in your doctor's and/or your physiotherapist's waiting room, and you will probably have had several discussions with an orthopaedic surgeon (a specialist in the treatment of bone ailments) or a neurosurgeon (a specialist in nerve defects).

Depending on the problem, the specialist may suggest one of many operations. The following are among the most common:

1. **Laminectomy** involves removing a small amount of bone from a part of the vertebra. This widens the hole in the spinal canal without weakening the spine itself. A day after the operation, you will be shown exercises to get your spine moving again. Indeed, if you don't get up and move about soon after a laminectomy, you may clog up your spine with clotting blood. An increase in pain, following the operation, could mean that there is a hidden joint problem or that there is excessive scar tissue.

2. **Spinal fusion** has a high-tech ring about it. Put simply, it is the surgical joining of one vertebra to another to stabilise the joint. Sometimes it's performed at the same time as a laminectomy. Spinal fusion may cure one problem, but it can create others. Somewhere along the line, the body will have to compensate for the immobility of the fused section. As with a laminectomy,

scar tissue and excessive bone growth can create new problems.

3. The **enzyme chymopapain** can be used to shrink a bulging disc. A pawpaw derivative is injected into the disc to dissolve harmful material and take pressure off the nerve root. A common side effect is persistent back pain for several weeks after the operation. In rare cases, the patient may have a dangerous allergic reaction.

4. In a **percutaneous posterolateral discectomy**, the centre of the offending disc is sucked out through a tiny hole. The efficacy of this procedure has not been proven and, for this reason, some surgeons have abandoned its use.

Pre-Operative Precautions

Certain procedures are carried out prior to any back operation. Checks may include an electrocardiogram to assess your heart function, a pulmonary function test to gauge the strength of your lungs, a urine test, a check to determine possible allergic reactions, nose and throat swabs taken and your skin examined for any inflammation, cuts or sores. Pulse, temperature and blood pressure are, of course, also taken.

On the more passive side of things, you will be instructed on being turned in bed every couple of hours after the operation, and may be measured for a lumbar corset and antiembolic stockings, which are often worn after back surgery to avoid blood-clotting in the legs. A physiotherapist will also prepare you for post-operative breathing and leg exercises.

Post-Operative Procedures

Anyone who has ever undergone surgery will be familiar with the recovery-room routine. After a back operation, you wake to find you have been fitted with some temporary apparatus which may be alarming if you are not prepared for it. There will be drainage tubes from the wound (removed a day or two after surgery), one from the bladder (removed approximately three days later) and possibly one from the hip, if a bone graft was necessary.

Since you are not permitted to eat or drink for the first day after the operation, an intravenous drip (I.V.) is inserted in the arm to provide the body with nourishment. A second, pain-killing I.V. may also be used. A tube inserted through the nose and into the stomach is used to drain excess stomach fluids until normal bowel function is restored. Any nausea is kept under control with injections.

All of the above are standard parts of the recovery procedure. Things start getting back to normal within 48 hours, when light food can be taken.

Stitches are removed within 10 to 12 days, and deep breathing and back exercises begin early, to prevent complications and to promote good blood circulation. The hospital will provide you with an appropriate exercise programme, but it is your responsibility to ensure the exercises are done when required and on an on-going basis.

Dizziness is quite common after such an operation, but eases up after just a few days. Walking frames and crutches are only used for a few days, if at all. A corset or brace is often used to protect the spine.

A physiotherapist is on hand to advise on comfortable, safe movement, and an occupational therapist will instruct on dressing, showering, toileting and future work and recreational habits.

After a few days of lying flat, with turns in the bed every couple of hours, patients are able to sit. The doctor will advise on the best types of chairs and the recommended posture when using them, but remember a firm chair with a high back is preferable, and bean bags and bucket seats, which do not provide proper support, should be avoided.

It is best to steer clear of lifting anything heavy for two or three months after surgery. Driving is usually possible after four to six weeks. This will depend on your individual rate of recovery.

Generally, gently does it for six to twelve weeks after the operation and, of course, healthy back habits, as outlined in this book, are recommended for continuing fitness.

Chapter 4
The Hands-On Approach

After attempting to give you some temporary relief from pain, your doctor will probably refer you to a physiotherapist – a health professional who has done years of study in the field of joint malfunction. Physiotherapists, like doctors, have their specialties, so make sure you are referred to one with a special interest in backs. If your injury is related to a sporting activity, you may prefer to consult a sports-injury specialist.

From the moment you walk into the physiotherapist's office, he or she will be watching the way you walk, sit and stand and, like your doctor, will ask you a lot of questions about your medical history, your lifestyle and your pain.

The physiotherapist will take note of your spinal movements while you bend, straighten and turn. Next, your muscles will be tested for function and your spine palpated, which means it is carefully pushed and prodded, to identify the source of your pain and any sign of tension or tenderness.

Your physiotherapist's first concern will be to minimise your discomfort, and the second to help the injury heal. He or she will then provide information so that you can consider lifestyle changes to stop the same thing happening again.

FACT FILE

House Calls

If you are incapacitated by pain, physiotherapists do make house calls. They will take steps to relieve your agony and leave you with hope for on-going relief. This hope comes in the form of gentle exercises which can be done at home. Contact the Chartered Society of Physiotherapy for details of local physiotherapists (see 'Helpful Addresses', page 83).

SEVEN STEPS TO CONSIDER

One or a combination of the following approaches may be recommended:

1. Rest
2. Heat and ice
3. Electrotherapy
4. Traction
5. Hydrotherapy
6. Manipulation and mobilisation
7. Remedial exercises

REST

Bed rest is sometimes suggested for a few days in the early stages of a back injury, while the initial swelling and inflammation dies down. A good example is a severely bulging disc. But, since inactivity does nothing for stiff joints, you will be advised to be up and moving your back again as soon as possible.

HEAT AND ICE

Heat and ice are used by physiotherapists to treat pain. Both can also be used at home when pain attacks, but you have to know when to choose heat and when to choose cold.

Ice tends to be most effective in the first 12 hours after an injury, to minimise inflammation. As a rough guide, if there's a possibility of bruising or swelling, as with a torn ligament, use an ice pack (which is available from pharmacies and which can double as a heat pack) or even a packet of frozen vegetables from the freezer (marked 'not to be eaten').

For spasms, use heat from an infra-red heat lamp, an electric blanket or heat pad, a hot water bottle wrapped in a cloth, or a heat pack. Be careful not to burn your skin or to use heat where you have already tried a rub-on ointment. If you suffer from chronic back pain, you probably already know that a very warm bath or shower can help to ease your discomfort.

ELECTROTHERAPY

A Transcutaneous Electrical Nerve Stimulation (TENS) machine is a small, battery-powered generator which transmits electrical impulses to pads placed on trouble spots on the back. It is thought that TENS works in a similar way to acupuncture, by blocking pain signals to the brain. The machine is small enough to wear on a belt, so you can move about. Interferential machines work in a similar way, using medium, rather than low-frequency current.

Ultrasound is another form of electrotherapy which has achieved good results in reducing pain. A handle attached to the ultrasound generator is moved around the affected area. There are two settings: one pulsed, for micro massage, the other continuous, for heating.

Lasers use infra-red light energy to increase cell activity and help speed healing in the early stages after an injury. The laser pencil is moved around on the affected area or held on acupuncture points.

TRACTION

Traction stretches the spine and encourages blood circulation. It passively exercises both problem and healthy areas. It does not target specific joints, but can be useful in reducing swelling that has not responded to other treatments. You lie on your back, side or stomach on a special traction table. The physiotherapist attaches a harness around your chest and another around your hips. A weight, which is carefully adjusted according to the desired effect, gently pulls on the spine.

If you suffer from a chronically stiff back and joint degeneration, your physio might suggest high-weight traction combined with a series of exercises for you to do at home.

HYDROTHERAPY

Hydrotherapy, as the name suggests, is treatment using water. The idea is that your body weight will be supported, taking pressure off the joints, in the warm water of a pool, usually located in a hospital or rehabilitation centre. The physiotherapist may suggest hydrotherapy if you cannot exercise your joints by yourself because of severe pain and stiffness. For the first sessions, the physiotherapist may enter the pool to teach you specific joint-releasing exercises, which you will then be able to continue on your own.

MANIPULATION AND MOBILISATION

Manipulation, mobilisation and massage are manual-pressure techniques used by physiotherapists to restore free movement to the joints. Your physiotherapist will make sure you have had a medical examination to rule out any potential troubles with his or her technique.

Manipulative physiotherapists help to relieve back pain by moving or adjusting the individual joints of the spine. The movements are very specific, targeting an area defined by thorough examination.

Manipulation should not cause pain. Your physiotherapist will ask you to lie down or sit on the treatment table. When you are in a relaxed state, firm pressure will be exerted, often using leverage, which can result in a surprising cracking sound. Don't worry – this is not the sound of your bones grinding back into place, but is thought to be the sound of a gas bubble forming in the fluid which lubricates the joints. Unfortunately, manipulation does not work for everyone.

Passive mobilisation can be used on its own or in conjunction with manipulation to achieve joint freedom and pain relief. You will be asked to lie face down on the treatment table while the therapist assesses your spine and identifies trouble spots. Work will then begin on those malfunctioning joints; they will be prised gently, but firmly, with thumbs or elbow. This does a lot to relieve stiffness and discomfort. Depending on the extent of your problem, you may need anything from one treatment to several weeks of treatment.

REMEDIAL EXERCISES

Whichever technique is used, the therapist will also recommend some exercises for you to continue at home (see Chapters 5 and 6). These exercises may well prevent a recurrence of your problem.

Physiotherapy is available on the NHS, but there can be a long wait, and session availability may be limited. You may wish to pay for private physiotherapy to ensure immediate and frequent treatment. Ask your GP for details.

FACT FILE

Manipulative Physiotherapy

Manipulative physiotherapy is a relatively new marriage of healing techniques. Like all physiotherapists, manipulative physiotherapists use passive mobilisation and a wide range of techniques, such as electrotherapy, massage and exercise. Among the conditions they treat are arthritis, disc disorders, shoulder pain and 'locked joints', such as wry neck. Contact the Chartered Society of Physiotherapy (see page 83) for further details.

WHEN GETTING BETTER MAKES YOU FEEL WORSE

The first steps on the road to recovery are to
relieve pain, reduce inflammation, and get
mobile. Then comes the hard part. It's true
that exerting pressure on the joints to get them
moving freely can cause its own pain, even
bruising. The experts call this treatment soreness. The good news is that this short-lived
discomfort will, in the long run, do you good.
Honestly! Your back specialist is trying to help
you.

Chapter 5
Back to Basics

There is no single set of back exercises that will suit all back-pain sufferers. Only someone such as a physiotherapist, who is trained in identifying specific trouble points, can prescribe a routine especially for you, after assessing the strength of important muscle groups – the hip flexors, abdominals and gluteal (bottom) muscles, for instance. At the same time, there are a few basic exercises which can help, particularly in the case of low back pain.

When the choice is between pain and ease of movement, the willpower to do these exercises follows naturally. Apart from that, you need little or no special equipment.

DON'T OVERDO IT

Exercise is great in the long term, but don't try to carry on regardless or push through the pain barrier. You may feel like a hero, but you will only slow down the healing process. Always check with your doctor before embarking on any exercise programme, especially if you are getting on in years.

Apart from these specific exercises, keep a good standard of overall fitness. Fitness means maintaining your body's functions in good working order – everything from your immune system to your strength, co-ordination and stamina.

As a rough guide to your fitness level, ask yourself this question: Am I exhausted at the end of the day? If the answer is yes, you need to alter your lifestyle. Among your goals for improving your general fitness should be:

1. Stop smoking.
2. Eat a good, mixed diet, covering all the major food groups.
3. Moderate your alcohol intake.
4. Reduce stress.
5. Fit some aerobic exercise into your day.

DO *NOT* EXERCISE IF:

1. Your injury is very recent. Consult your doctor.
2. Any of these exercises cause the pain to worsen. Stop immediately and consult your doctor or therapist.
3. You feel leg pain, tingling or numbness.

BASIC BACK MOVES

The aim of these exercises is to:

- Increase your general flexibility.
- Mobilise your spine.
- Strengthen the muscle groups which support your back.
- Stretch tight joints, muscles and ligaments.
- Improve your posture.

Lower Back Stretches

(a) Lie down on a carpeted floor or mat – not on a bed. With your arms stretched out on either side, lift both knees to your chest and hold for a moment to stretch your lower back. Keeping your feet off the ground, slowly roll both knees to one side, head facing in the opposite direction to the knees. Don't allow the shoulders to lift off the ground. Hold for 10 seconds, and repeat on the other side. Repeat four or five times to relieve stiffness.

(b) In the same starting position, extend one leg and bend the other knee. Hook your foot under the knee of the straight leg. Roll your knee over, without lifting your shoulders. Hold for 20 seconds, looking in the opposite direction. Change sides and repeat.

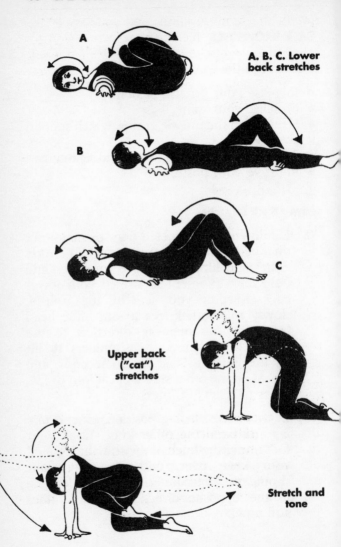

A. B. C. Lower back stretches

Upper back ("cat") stretches

Stretch and tone

(c) In the same position, pull your knees up, keeping your feet on the ground and together. Gently roll your knees from one side to the other, getting a good spinal stretch. Don't hold. As you roll, turn your head to face in the opposite direction to your knees. Roll about 10 times to each side.

Important: For passive stretches of the lower back, see 'Emergency Measures', page 46.

Upper Back Stretch

In the 'cat stretch', the starting position is on the hands and knees, with the knees comfortably apart. With head down, tuck your bottom under and raise your back, pulling in your tummy muscles as you do so. Come back to a flat back, head up. Don't arch downwards. Repeat five times.

Stretch and Tone

In the cat stretch position, bring one knee to your chest and your forehead to your knee, then stretch the same leg straight out behind you, parallel to the floor – do not raise or lower this leg. Curl back in again. Repeat, slowly, five times. On the last stretch, extend your leg and lift the opposite arm, stretching out your fingers. Hold for five seconds. Repeat the whole routine on the opposite side. This strengthens the back and balances the muscles.

FACT FILE

Save Your Back

For minimum back strain, it's important to move safely from lying to standing. Roll on to one side, come to a sitting position, kneel on one knee, then push, using your leg muscles, to stand.

TUMMY TIGHTENERS

The abdominal or stomach muscles are perhaps the most important group to work out if you suffer from low back pain. Without strong abdominals, your stomach will stick out, pulling your spine forward. Try the following simple routine.

(a) Lie on your back with your knees bent and your feet flat on the floor, shoulder-width apart. Place your hands behind your head, elbows back. Tilt your pelvis, as described in 'Take Care!' (page 44), take a breath in and lift your chest towards the ceiling as you breathe out. This is a small movement – do not curl up. Be guided by your own strength, and stop when you feel your muscles begin to quiver.

(b) This one is more difficult. Lie on your back, knees bent, feet flat on the floor. With your hands behind the head, elbows flat, as before, breathe in, raise one knee to the opposite elbow, keeping your other elbow flat. Straighten the bent knee without replacing your foot on the floor, at the same time lifting your other knee to the opposite elbow. The action is somewhat like bicycling without the circular motion.

This is a rhythmic exercise which appears gentle but is very effective. The slower you go and the lower you take your legs, the harder you work your muscles. As you build up strength, hold between changeovers.

HOME-WORKER'S CHECKLIST

Housework is responsible for many back troubles. The following tips help avoid problems:

- Put a lot of variety into your day. Don't spend too long dusting the skirting boards for instance. Do a little at a time.
- Never try to move any heavy furniture on your own.
- Squat or kneel to work at a low level, such as when making the bed.
- When sweeping or vacuuming, use short strokes, bend your knees and move your feet to avoid over-reaching.
- When you have to stand for prolonged periods, put one leg on a higher level: for instance, when you do the dishes, open a cupboard door and put your foot on a shelf.
- Take special care when loading the dishwasher. Kneel or bend from the knee, with back straight and chin parallel to the floor.

- Keep in mind the basic principles of standing, sitting and lifting (see Chapter 6).

GENTLY DOES IT

When you feel pain or stiffness coming on, try the following gentle movements. In fact, do them anyway, whether you suffer from back-ache or not, to help prevent you becoming one of the 90 per cent of people who will suffer from disc disorders.

These are great refreshers. Use them in work rest breaks, when gardening, driving long distances or between shots on the golf course.

FACT FILE

Take Care!
To perform any sit-up type of exercises without damaging your back, bend your knees and tilt the pelvis so that your lower back is resting flat against the floor before you lift. Never do straight-leg sit-up exercises or try to pull the body up to a sitting position, even with the legs bent. 'Crunches' or curl-ups are just as effective and much safer. Pregnant women should always support their stomach muscles when performing crunches. They do this by crossing their arms and placing their hands on the lower rib cage, drawing the muscles towards the centre, and holding.

---

1. For the neck

All of these movements are to be done smoothly and slowly, without pausing and with no sudden twisting. If you are in pain, you may have to support your head in your hands.

Seated, chin parallel to the floor, move your head to look over your right shoulder, then your left. Repeat. Now look down, then up, twice. Next, bend your head to one side, bringing your ear towards your shoulder, then to the other side. Repeat.

2. For the mid-back

Hold your tummy muscles in throughout. Stand with your feet shoulder-width apart. Elbows bent, lift your arms to shoulder level, then press your elbows back gently. At the point of resistance, push your chest forward. Repeat.

As before, elbows bent, arms at shoulder level, twist gently to the right, hold the stretch. Twist gently to the left. Hold. Repeat.

Stretch your arms towards the ceiling, fingers straight. First, pull up with one hand, then with the other, as if you were trying to touch the ceiling, about 10 times.

3. For the lower back

Stand with your feet shoulder-width apart. Fingers pointed out towards your waist, place your thumbs on either side of your spine. Arch backwards gently to the point of resistance, pressing your thumbs into your back as you do so. Repeat.

YOGA FOR BACKS

A couple of decades ago, those who practised yoga were regarded as part of a counter-culture. Today, a lot of people in nine-to-five jobs have discovered the benefits of this ancient Indian exercise system.

Using positions developed two and a half centuries ago (nothing much has changed in the human body in all that time), the yoga instructor can teach you how to maintain flexible joints for the rest of your life. During a good class, you will mobilise most of your major joints and many you didn't know you had, while strengthening and stretching your muscles and ligaments. And you will hardly realise you are exercising.

You can learn yoga from a book, but there's a risk that you may not practise the positions effectively or safely. It's best to find a teacher by word of mouth or through the Yellow Pages. You can take up yoga – after consulting your doctor, of course – at any age or level of fitness.

EMERGENCY MEASURES

Back pain is unpredictable. It may strike out of the blue, when you can't get immediate medical attention. For low back pain, many physiotherapists recommend a first-aid routine developed by New Zealand physiotherapist Robin McKenzie.

Step 1 Lie face down on the floor with your head to one side, and relax completely for five minutes. If pain stops you doing even this, go directly to bed and lie flat on your back, using a rolled-up towel for support around your waist. Have another try the following day.

Step 2 When you can lie like this quite comfortably, do 10 of the following exercises every two hours. The theory is that, if bending forward caused your backache, bending backwards may cure it. Expect a slight increase in pain at first.

• Lying face down, place your elbows under your shoulders, supporting yourself on your forearms. Take a few deep breaths to encourage total relaxation. Stay in this position for about five minutes.

• Return to your flat position. Place your hands under your shoulders, as if you were about to do a press-up. Relax the lower half of your body completely, letting your lower back sag. Now, straighten your elbows and push the top half of your body up as far as pain allows. Maintain for a few seconds and return to the starting position. Each time you do this, try to push your body a little higher.

Step 3 If the pain persists and seems to be more on one side than the other, roll hips slightly away from the painful side and try the exercises in Step 2 again.

**Exercises to relieve lower back pain: if bending
forward caused backache, bending backwards –
as in these modified 'pushups' – may cure it**

Step 4 Rest as much as possible, with correct
low back and neck support.

Step 5 Avoid bending forward for several days.

Step 6 When you must sit, use a lumbar roll
(see Chapter 8).

Chapter 6
Five Steps to a Healthy Back

Make sure you are one of those who beat back pain by maintaining a good posture. This is not a matter of being able to walk with a book balanced on your head, as you might have been taught in earlier days; it's holding the body in a way that maintains its healthy, natural curves. Good posture has many hidden benefits, not the least of which is a pain-free back.

STEP I: STAND TALL

By standing tall, you will increase your lung capacity, improve your circulation and allow your internal organs to work more efficiently. You will also look and feel better.

When standing, don't force your shoulders back, but simply lift up your chest. Your chin will follow to its natural position, parallel to the floor. When you 'think tall', you put less strain on the tiny bones of the neck which support your heavy head. Keep your stomach and buttock muscles pulled tight to stop that low back curve from becoming exaggerated. Weak stomach muscles are a major cause of disc problems.

Carry your weight forward (rather than backwards) on the balls of your feet, which should be slightly apart and pointing slightly outwards. As you walk along, get out of the habit of looking down at the ground.

STEP 2: SIT PRETTY

Standing still puts a lot of strain on your spine, but not as much as sitting does. If you spend much of your day hunched in front of paper-work or a computer monitor, you won't be doing your back a favour.

The first priority is a good chair (see Chapter 8) which will support your lower back. Sit right back in it with your feet touching the floor or on a footstool. Use a small cushion or lumbar (low back) roll to support the curve of the lower back.

Also adjust your car seat so that you can sit upright without stretching to reach the steering wheel or pedals. On long trips, use a lumbar support. The same applies to long flights; take a lumbar support with you, or improvise with a firmly rolled-up towel or blanket.

Have you ever watched someone suffering from a disc problem getting out of a chair? They come to standing bent over their desks before straightening up, painfully. Don't let your back even approach this level of stiffness – take frequent breaks to walk around and stretch. Never throw yourself into a chair; it is better to keep your back straight as you sit down gently, controlling your speed with your leg muscles. To protect your back when getting out of a chair, you should place your feet comfortably apart and move your bottom towards the seat edge, before pushing off, using your thigh muscles.

DRIVER'S CHECKLIST

People who drive for a living report three times as much disc trouble as other workers.

- Don't drive long distances without hourly rest and exercise breaks. Not only will you be a safer driver, you'll arrive at your destination loose-jointed and happy.
- Don't carry your wallet in a back pocket. Over time, the small imbalance the extra padding causes can create painful problems in the spine.
- Modern car seats are often built with lumbar and neck support – make sure yours is adjusted to suit you, or invest in a lumbar insert.
- Sit far enough back from the steering wheel so that your arms are almost straight.

STEP 3: ONE, TWO, THREE – LIFT

Lifting causes a large proportion of industrial back injuries. It's also a common cause of back pain around the house, especially for mothers, who are constantly picking up babies and heavy shopping loads. Next time you get the chance, watch a weightlifter in action. Back injury would effectively put an end to his career. To prevent it, he:

1. Stands with his feet comfortably apart, about shoulder width.
2. Gets as close to the weight as possible.
3. Keeps his back as straight as possible.
4. Tucks in his chin and tightens his stomach muscles.
5. Bends deeply at the knees, using the strong leg muscles to lift in one smooth movement.

Apart from teaching you how to lift correctly and assessing your strengths and weaknesses, your physiotherapist can advise you on making your workplace or home a safer place. Here are a few changes you can make right now:

- Use mechanical help, such as a crane or forklift, wherever possible.
- Ask for help – two sets of muscles are better than one.
- Store heavy goods at waist height to minimise bending.

- Don't lift heavy loads higher than your waist.
- Don't lift or carry uneven loads.

The wrong way to lift   The right way to lift

STEP 4: FIT, NOT FAT

If you are a bit overweight but fit, the extra baggage won't affect your back. Excess weight on a couch potato puts a strain not only on the heart but the spine, too. Ask your doctor to recommend a diet you can live with. Walking is one of the all-time great fat burners.

STEP 5: STRESS MANAGEMENT

Stress is the bugbear of modern living. Life would be very dull without the occasional surge of adrenalin which stress produces, but too much can cause not only emotional problems but increased muscle tension, leading to spasm. A lot of us carry tension in our necks and shoulders, which inevitably reflects in low back pain. The first step is to pinpoint harmful stress in your life and consider ways to banish or, at least, minimise it.

Many community health centres now offer stress management classes, or your family doctor may be able to refer you to a meditation or self-hypnosis instructor or a pain clinic where you will learn relaxation techniques (see Chapter 3).

One effective and popular method of unwinding from the day's stresses is known as progressive relaxation. Once you have tried it, you may become addicted. You can buy tapes which will lead you through this routine, or take instruction from a psychologist or other stress counsellor.

The method is based on the fact that you are probably so used to muscular tension that you are completely unaware of it. The aim is to get you out of the habit.

Lie down in a darkened room. Beginning with the toes, progressively tense, hold and relax every part of your body. Your stress counsellor will guide you, saying something like this: 'Tense your toes, hold that tension, now let go. Feel the difference.' You may be asked to use a word such as 'calm', which you can say or think on an out-breath. You will begin to associate this word with muscular relaxation and you can use it in situations when you can't go through the whole routine, such as driving in heavy traffic.

A continuation of this form of relaxation, which is similar to self-hypnosis, is guided imagery. Here, the therapist may ask you to imagine a garden or other restful and beautiful place where you feel happy and secure. You will walk down the stairs into the garden and imagine the flowers, the smells, the sun warming your face. At the end of the session, you will mentally walk back up the stairs and gradually come back to reality before opening your eyes.

Studies show that a 20-minute session of this type of deep relaxation is the equivalent of two and a half hours' sleep.

Exercise is, in itself, an excellent stress-beater but should be combined with a more gentle therapy – a long stretch class, at the very least. Are you the type of person who can't sit still long enough to meditate? You might be better to take up karate or Tai-chi to deal with your inner tension.

Chapter 7
Putting Your Back into Sport

It's trendy to participate in sport. So trendy, in fact, that we have become slightly brainwashed – we tend to believe that all sport must be good for us. Well, it's true that regular exercise can work wonders. It strengthens the cardiovascular system (heart, lungs and circulation), increases flexibility and relieves stress. On the down side, fast and furious sports that use joint-grinding, repetitive movements are hard on the skeleton.

You are asking for injury if you sit or drive around all day, then have a sudden burst of activity in the evening – an hour on the squash court, say, or pounding the pavement – without a decent warm-up before and warm-down afterwards.

Don't use those warnings as an excuse not to get fit. You can adapt almost any sport so that it doesn't do lasting damage to your spine. With body awareness, it may even do some good. Moderation, as in so many of life's enjoyable pursuits, is the key.

The following advice assumes that you are already having problems with your back. Ask your physiotherapist for specific strengthening and flexibility exercises, which will give you maximum enjoyment of your chosen leisure pursuit.

WALKING

Where jogging has been losing popularity, walking has been gaining. It has many of the same benefits, including excellent fat-burning qualities, without the unwanted side effects.

All you need to start is a pair of well-fitting, sturdy shoes, comfortable clothing and wet weather gear, if necessary, and off you go. To do your back some good while you walk, stand tall, with your spine straight, walk rhythmically using long strides and swing your arms, with your elbows slightly bent, in the direction you're travelling.

WATER SPORTS

Swimming is a good all-round sport with cardiovascular and strengthening benefits. Swimming freestyle extends the spine, so it's a boon if your back pain stems from disc problems.

However, if your back trouble is caused by excessive curvature in the lower spine (lumbar lordosis) your back may sag when you swim freestyle or breaststroke. As with all sports, stop immediately if you experience pain.

Aquarobics – exercise in water, sometimes to music – is gaining a strong following, especially among those who don't like the sometimes jarring pace of land-bound aerobics. It's suitable for pregnant women and most people suffering from joint problems, as the water supports your body weight.

AEROBICS

Methods of teaching aerobics have changed a lot in the last few years. No longer are we encouraged to 'go for the burn'. Now, high-intensity, low-impact exercise is offered by most good gyms. Stay clear of high-impact jumping and fast-paced twisting or bending.

All in all, aerobics provide a good workout for the joints. It's up to you to take it easy until your body is ready to keep up with the class stars.

JOGGING

Still hugely popular, jogging is losing a lot of ground to less stressful sports. Runners are literally grinding to a halt. Every time your foot hits the ground, the impact sends a shock wave through your skeleton. It's not surprising that, after a few years, your joints begin to protest against the abuse. Physiotherapists treat thousands of running-related knee and back problems.

On the positive side, jogging is great aerobic exercise and a first-class stress reliever. If you must run, slip on a pair of good shock-absorbing shoes and head for your nearest grassy park or paddock. Avoid concrete surfaces, and take time to do a thorough stretch and warm-up routine before your run and stretch and warm-down routine after. Ignore this advice at your peril.

BALL GAMES

Golf is a wonderfully relaxing game. Unfortunately, it's just too one-sided and involves too much standing around and bending to be good for your spine. The walks between shots are fine. All this probably won't make you give up the sport – unless, of course, you have already been immobilised by back injury. Instead, do a series of exercises to compensate for all the swinging on your 'playing' side: slow twisting, extending, arching (see 'Gently Does It', Chapter 5). Remember to pull the tummy muscles in, especially while standing waiting for your partner to play, and to bend from the knees or squat when picking up the ball.

No sport that knocks the body about in the way that rugby does can be good for your spine. Soccer, however, with its relative lack of body-breaking contact and its free-ranging movements, can do the spine some good. Cricket and bowling, like golf, involve a lot of standing about and bending – strong stomach and back muscles are a must.

RACQUET SPORTS

Sorry to break this to you, but tennis is not good for the spine. Not as bad as squash, though, with all that high-speed twisting and turning. Both sports use a lot of repetitive movements and sudden lunges, which put particular stress on the lower back. If you do a lot of exercises to strengthen your stomach, back and leg muscles, and make a decent stretch and warm-up session a habit, you can get away with a bit of social tennis and squash.

ATHLETE'S CHECKLIST

- Warm up and warm down before and after exercise.
- Stretch before and after exercise.
- Wear well-fitting shoes designed for your sport.
- Condition your body specifically, especially for seasonal sports such as skiing and tennis.
- Allow an injury to heal before jumping back into your chosen activity.
- Ask your physiotherapist or sport instructor to check that your style of exercising is not putting unnecessary strain on your back.

RICE and HARM

If you engage in any active sport or hobby, you should know about RICE and HARM.

RICE is used for injuries where there's a risk of bruising and/or swelling. It stands for:

- Rest.
- Ice: Applied for 10 minutes every hour to start with.
- Compression: Bandage the area firmly, but not too tightly, to control swelling.
- Elevation: Raise the injured part, if possible, to help drainage of fluids.

Just as it suggests, HARM warns you of what to avoid after an injury. Remember that:

- Heat increases bleeding.
- Alcohol increases swelling.
- Running or high activity can make an injury worse.
- Massage on the first day can increase both swelling and bleeding.

Chapter 8
Back Rest: Making Life Easier

The high incidence of back pain has not been lost on inventors, innovators and manufacturers. There's a wide range of goods on the market that can help you ease or prevent backache and generally make life at home and in the workplace more comfortable. It is worth shopping around when buying bedding, seating and work surfaces.

A GOOD NIGHT'S SLEEP

Most people, including health professionals, have long maintained that the best mattress has just enough 'give' to mould to the natural curve of the spine. People tend to move less on a soft mattress, and immobility is, of course, the enemy of stiff joints. All muscles have what is called 'jelling time' – the time it takes them to stiffen from staying in one position too long. The older you are, the shorter your jelling time.

If you wake up in the morning free from aches and pains, you probably have a good bed.

If not, experiment with putting the mattress on the floor or laying it on a couple of flat boards.

It's also possible you are choosing a sleep position that causes discomfort. Lying on your stomach puts stress on your neck and lower back. If you naturally move on to your stomach during the night and experience pain, place a pillow under your hips. Conversely, if sleeping on your back causes pain, slip a pillow under your knees. It's difficult to control sleep positions, as we move frequently during the night.

When buying a mattress, swallow your embarrassment and lie down on it for at least five minutes, preferably longer, with your partner, if possible. On the right mattress, you should not roll in towards each other. Choose an innerspring or rubber mattress on a solid, rather than a wire, base.

PILLOWS

Surprisingly little scientific research has been done into what makes a good pillow, yet there are dozens of 'therapeutic' pillows on the market. Commonsense tells us that, if you put your neck in a position which stretches the nerve fibres in your soft tissues, they will begin to ache.

When you are young and mobile, you can lie on your tummy with your head turned and you won't be at the end of your stretching range – in other words, you could turn your head even further. As you grow older, the limits are narrower.

Unfortunately, you won't feel the pain until you come out of the stretch. You may not notice it until you try to move and experience pain. If you sleep on your tummy with a pillow pushing your head backwards, you further tighten the neck muscles. What you need is a sleep position and pillow which will support your neck comfortably without causing overstretching.

Young people can be quite comfortable lying flat on the floor. An older person's neck is stiffer and just won't go back. Therefore, they need a pillow that supports the head in a forward position, which will tuck well in and accommodate the arched position of the neck.

If you usually lie on your back, you need a pillow that is not too fat and will mould to the shape of your neck. If you sleep on your side and have a stiff neck through ageing and disability, you need a fairly fat pillow to support your head.

There are a number of therapeutic pillows available which you may find useful.

If you are a back sleeper, you would place the firmly padded section under your neck, with your head in the middle section. A side sleeper would turn it around to use the wider, medium-density section under the neck so that the head drops into the middle section. The aim is to support your muscles in a neutral position.

Generally speaking, you need a flat, non-rubber pillow which supports and moulds into your neck. Ask your physiotherapist for advice.

SEATING ARRANGEMENTS

It may come as a surprise that sitting puts more strain on your spine than standing. There are hundreds of chairs on the market, yet most of them pay scant attention to the design of the human spine.

In an office chair, look for firm upholstery which allows you to support most of your weight on your large pelvic bones. The seat should slope slightly from back to front and be just high enough so that your thighs are at right angles to your lower legs when your feet are resting flat on the floor. The best chairs can be adapted to suit your height but, if the seat is too high, use a footrest.

Lumbar or low back support is another consideration. Spend a lot of time sitting in chairs before you decide on the right one for you. A chair should allow you to maintain the three natural curves of your back. Slowly but surely, designers of conventional office chairs are taking all these factors into consideration.

Watch children kneeling on the floor. They naturally lean back on their heels with a straight back and relaxed stomach muscles. This is long before their posture gets into bad adult habits. The Norwegian 'Balans' chair was developed to allow adults to sit in this same childlike pose, with the weight of the body supported by the knees and the normal spinal curves preserved.

There are many versions of the Balans chair, but they may not be the answer to every seat-bound back-sufferer's prayer. To feel comfortable, you should already have the good posture and strong muscular support system of a horse-rider. Before you buy, test out one of these chairs for two or three weeks, if possible. They are certainly not for everyone.

The worst kind of sofa is one that many people think is the most comfortable: the low, soft, squashy couch you sink into. Like the office chair, a sofa should be fairly firm, with good lumbar support and at a height which allows you to sit well back, with your feet resting on the floor.

In cars, the driver's seat should have firm upholstery with a slight backward tilt and some lateral support. The back rest should contain a lumbar support at the correct height for you. If not, you should buy or improvise a lumbar support.

WORK SURFACES

For office work, the desktop should be at the level of the elbows when seated so that the forearm is horizontal when writing. It's generally better to sit low, as this puts less strain on the lower back, but for some people a high position will be better.

Clerical workers should follow the example of artists and architects, who generally use a sloping work surface, relieving strain on the shoulders and upper back. There are several adjustable tilted desk attachments on the market.

You should not have to bend over to work at kitchen benchtops or ironing boards, and your elbow should, again, be at right angles to the work surface.

LOW BACK SUPPORTS

The most common back pain is felt in the low back or lumbar spine. For that reason, there are dozens of low back supports on the market, all of which will encourage your aim of lifelong good posture.

One of the most widely used is the lumbar roll, a small cylindrical pillow which can be strapped to the back rest of most seats. The roll effectively stops you slouching with a rounded back. Use it when you are watching television, driving or reading, as well as working.

As your muscles adapt to unfamiliar good posture, you may feel a whole new range of aches and pains. Don't throw away the roll – the pains will diminish until you can no longer sit slouched without feeling uncomfortable.

Lumbar corsets are frowned upon for long-term use because they may do the work of weak back muscles. However, for temporary relief and support during the initial stages of a painful attack, they are a godsend. The stiff corset works by acting as a self-powered heat pad, limiting the movement of the back and transmitting the load to the abdomen.

OFFICE-WORKER'S CHECKLIST

- Sit up straight and also move about frequently.
- Use a sloping desk or a document holder, if necessary, to avoid constant bending when using a typewriter or computer monitor.
- Take exercise breaks: walk around, do a few simple exercises.
- Arrange your work space so that the most frequently used items are within easy reach, to avoid a lot of bending and stretching.
- Don't cradle the telephone between your neck and shoulder.

BITS AND PIECES

It's good to see so many schoolchildren using backpacks rather than carrying bags, full of heavy books, slung over one shoulder. Whatever you carry, hold it as close to the body as possible.

Wheels for luggage and trolleys for shopping also combat back strain. The suitcase must be high enough and the trolley must have long enough handles to avoid stooping when pushing or pulling.

Inversion machines mimic traction. The frames attach at the ankle and allow you to hang upside-down so that the vertebrae can pull apart, allowing you to relax while your joints benefit from a good flow of blood. Do not use traction frames or boots without consulting your doctor or physiotherapist. You may make things worse.

Posture wedges make sitting in straight-backed chairs much more comfortable by creating a seat which slopes from back to front.

Electric massagers are great aids for relaxing muscle spasms – wonderful if you can rope someone else into doing it for you. Unfortunately, it's hard to relax completely while trying to massage your own spine. A wooden roller device can be just as effective. One popular type is a curved stick with two balls at one end; the idea is that you lie on your back with the roller placed so that the balls are on either side of your spine. You now move up and down to create a massage effect. The movement, combined with the pressure of the rollers, can do a lot to free your spine. Again, ask a good mate to help out, or do it yourself.

Many of these products are available through back-specialist shops, or ask your doctor or physiotherapist.

Chapter 9
Back Chat on the Alternatives

Natural, drug-free healing is becoming more and more popular. In fact, where natural healing ends and traditional medicine begins is an increasingly grey area. For the person in the street, the differences between manipulative physiotherapists, osteopaths and chiropractors can be hard to pick. In some cases, it's a matter of philosophy, in others terminology or approach to finding out the cause of your pain. There is a school of thought which maintains that the personal attention and interest of this type of therapist does a lot to encourage healing. But a major consideration in choosing any healer is how much medical training that person has.

Both chiropractic and osteopathy fell into disrepute because of exaggerated claims that the treatments could cure almost any human ailment. Modern practitioners tend to stick to what they know best – manipulating the joints to ease pain. There is still a lot of controversy about the techniques used. As with all medical practices, the success rate depends on the individual.

No matter which back specialist you choose, he or she should be able to give you broad-ranging advice on preventing another attack. If this does not happen, find another practitioner.

You can attend a chiropractor or osteopath without a doctor's referral, but always see your doctor first to narrow down the cause of your backache.

OSTEOPATHY

Osteopathy was developed in the 1870s by a medical practitioner. The osteopath examines you from the toes up for signs of dysfunction, such as muscle tension or joint stiffness. In treatment, he or she will relax the muscles by careful stretching and massage, manipulating the affected joint until it moves freely. A treatment session may end with a high-speed thrust, using a variety of specialised techniques, sometimes resulting in that 'cracking' noise – thought to be the sound of a gas bubble forming when the joint capsule is stretched momentarily.

CHIROPRACTIC

Chiropractic is based on the belief that poor alignment of the spine can be responsible for many types of illness. Like osteopathy, it has been around for about a century. Its practitioners (called chiropractors) concentrate on manipulating the spine. When you visit a chiropractor, he or she should make a detailed study of your spinal alignment, including whether you have one leg shorter than the other or another structural or mechanical problem. The grand finale – a short, sharp thrust – can feel quite dramatic. Both osteopathy and chiropractic treatments can result in soreness, which should pass within a day or two.

MASSAGE

Where there is back pain, there is almost certainly muscle spasm and that's where high-quality therapeutic massage comes in. A good masseur will be able to ease your discomfort, and you can't knock that, but he or she won't be able to treat the underlying problem with massage alone. Massage may be used in combination with a technique known as moxibustion, in which small heated cups filled with herbs are used to draw blood to the affected area, helping to release the spasm.

Don't waste your and their time answering the massage advertisements in the classified section of your newspaper. Don't get me wrong – some could be genuine, but you won't find out for sure until you get there. Instead, ask your doctor or back specialist to recommend a practitioner. Deep-tissue massage is often used in conjunction with manipulative therapy by physiotherapists, chiropractors and osteopaths.

Almost every civilisation has developed its own massage technique. Thanks to our multi-cultural society, most are available in the UK.

ACUPUNCTURE

Many people report that their pain has been relieved after acupuncture. Certainly, it's worth a try. No one knows why sticking needles into a person's body should treat pain, but one theory says it stimulates the brain to release pain-killing hormones, called endorphins, into the blood-stream. However, just like pain-killing drugs, it may simply mask an underlying problem.

When you attend an acupuncturist, he or she will take your pulse in three positions in each hand, then proceed to insert acupuncture needles on the body's meridians, or energy lines, according to ancient Chinese practice. The sensation is one of mild to medium discomfort rather than pain. The needles used are generally disposable or will be retained for your sole use.

THE NEW AGE APPROACH

In pain studies, it's been found that believing a method will work plays a big part in its success. There's a wide variety of alternatives to pain-killing pills. Just a few are mentioned here.

Depending on your personality and beliefs, you may want to try hypnosis, reflexology (in which pressure points on the feet are massaged to relieve pain in other parts of the body), or psychic healing. Shiatsu is related to both massage and acupuncture. It involves exerting pressure on 'energy meridians', or nerve paths.

Rolfing, named after chemist Ida Rolf, is another type of massage, in which the muscles are manipulated very vigorously. If 'no pain, no gain' is your motto, this could be the therapy for you.

Both the Alexander Technique and the Feldenkrais Method teach specific exercises combined with lifestyle changes to achieve freedom of movement, which inevitably helps to prevent backache. There are several books on both methods and teaching centres in most major cities.

FACT FILE

Be Wary
Not all acupuncturists, chiropractors and osteopaths are registered in their profession. Therefore, before using (and paying for) their services, check that they are registered by contacting the relevant association. See 'Helpful Addresses', page 83, for addresses and telephone numbers.

Chapter 10
Turning Your Back on Myths

1. **'We are shorter standing up than we are lying down'**
It's a fact that we are slightly taller when we get up in the morning than we are at the end of the day. Astronauts can grow several centimetres after a few days of weightlessness.

2. **'We should be walking on four legs, not two'**
Maybe, maybe not, for even our four-legged friends can suffer from back problems. The dachshund, for instance, has a long, poorly supported spine. The spines of dinosaur skeletons show similar wear and tear to those of humans.

3. **'Not tonight, dear – my back's killing me'**
Back pain can stop you enjoying sex, but it can also be used as a means of avoidance. If you are ambivalent about sex, you may need relationship counselling. If your back pain is on the physical level, be assured; good quality sex, not too rough, but using plenty of hip and tummy action, will

strengthen your abdominal and buttock muscles, which, in turn, help to support your back. If sex makes your backache worse, discuss it with your doctor or physiotherapist, who may be able to suggest more comfortable positions, such as 'spoons' in which you both lie on your side. The answer could be something as simple as a pillow in the small of the back. Massage and spa baths both soothe tension and help you enjoy sex. Where there's a will, there's a way.

4. **'A friend recommended a mixture of garlic and vinegar for my bad back. After a couple of weeks on the mixture, the pain miraculously disappeared'**
There is no scientific proof that such 'wonder cures' do anything for backache, but by all means try them if it makes you feel better. The body has a natural healing time, usually about six to eight weeks. Most attacks of back pain get better without medical or other help.

5. **'I slept with the window open and woke up with a stiff neck'**
This has some truth. One theory is that sitting or sleeping in a draught can 'close down' the blood vessels and cut down the blood flow to the back, which, in turn, will cause stiffness and pain. Heat – a hot shower, hot-water bottle, heat pack, etc –

is worth trying for this sort of predicament.

6. **'My back feels worse just before my period'**
   This is not your imagination. The reason seems to be that women tend to retain fluid at this time, putting extra pressure on any back injury. Using tampons can cause low back pain.

7. **'In the old days, backache wasn't as common as it is today'**
   You have to go back a long way to prove this one. Modern man performs about 500 lifts a day, compared to Stone Age man's 50, so Neolithic skeletons show far less wear and tear. By the time we reached Victorian times, back-pain sufferers were beating a path to the door of 'bone setters' – forerunners of today's osteopaths and chiropractors.

8. **'I'm 1.9 metres tall and can't get rid of my backache'**
   Yes, tall people are more likely to suffer from backache than short people. This is a postural, not structural, problem, perhaps because tall people tend to bend more in day-to-day life.

9. **'A bad back's easy to fake, so it's a great way to avoid work'**
   Back pain has an unworthy reputation as a

tool for malingerers. There is even a term –
'compensation neurosis' – for the alleged
condition suffered by those awaiting finan-
cial compensation for back injury incurred
at work. The reputation may have come
about because it is not easy for a doctor to
narrow down the causes of back pain. Pain
felt in one region can be caused by an
injury in quite another part of the body,
transmitted via the thousands of nerves
that make up the spinal cord. It's true that
many work days are lost through back pain,
but statistics show that the complaint tends
to have very definite causes. Faked back
pain is far less common than some employ-
ers and stand-up comedians would have
you believe.

10. **'When things aren't going well, my back
    feels worse'**
    This is true. When you are generally con-
    tented or have something to look forward
    to, you don't feel pain as much as you do
    when you have suffered a disappointment.
    A positive attitude will help you beat pain.

Glossary

Abdominals: the four layers of stomach muscles.

Cervical vertebrae: the five bones of the neck.

Chiropractic: method of treatment based on the belief that poor alignment of the spine may cause many types of illness. Professional treatment involves manipulation.

Coccyx: the tail bone.

Disc degeneration: wearing down of the outer layers of the disc, which can result in the soft inner core bulging outwards.

Endorphins: pain-killing hormones released by the brain.

Hip flexors: muscles which help to bend the joint between the hip and upper leg.

Intervertebral discs: cushions of cartilage which separate the vertebrae. Each has a soft inner core surrounded by rings of tough fibres.

Kyphosis: abnormal outward bulge of the spine.

Lordosis: abnormal inward curve of the lower back.

Lesion: damage.

Ligaments: strong fibres which provide support for the joints.

Lumbar vertebrae: the seven bones of the lower back.

Osteopathy: method of treatment involving professional stretching and massage.

Sciatica: general description of a range of symptoms caused by irritation of the sciatic nerves.

Sciatic nerves: nerves that run from the lower back, across the buttocks and down the backs of the legs.

Scoliosis: Curvature of the spine to one side.

Spinal cord: a cable of nerves running from the brain through a canal in the centre of the spinal column.

Thoracic vertebrae: the 12 bones of the mid-back, or chest region.

Trauma: injury or the condition caused by injury.

Vertebrae: the 24 bones which form the spinal column.

Medication

Non-Steroidal Anti-Inflammatory Drugs

Ibuprofen (Brufen), naproxen (Naprosyn), piroxicam (Feldene) and many others.

Function: Used to control inflammation in arthritic diseases, such as rheumatoid arthritis, but also effective for some forms of back pain.

These drugs may produce unpleasant side effects such as nausea, headaches, dizziness and a rash, and are best taken with meals.

Never take these drugs without your doctor's advice and certainly don't use them if you suffer from a gastro-intestinal disease, such as a peptic ulcer or a bleeding disorder.

Pain Killers

Analgesics, such as paracetamol, can be used in most cases of back pain. More potent pain killers, such as codeine phosphate and other narcotics, are available only with a doctor's prescription. You can form a dependency on these medications.

Muscle Relaxants

The benzo-diazepine group, of which the best known is probably diazepam (such as Valium), can be used to reduce muscle spasm. These drugs cause drowsiness and poor coordination, so you should not drive or use machinery while using them. Your doctor will not prescribe diazepam if you have a respiratory complaint or a problem with drug addiction. These <u>must</u> only be used on a short-term basis.

Helpful Addresses

Listed below are a number of organisations that can help back pain sufferers in a variety of ways.

Association of Swimming Therapy
4 Oak Street
Shrewsbury
Salop
SY3 7RH
(01743) 344393

Backfriend
ME Design Ltd
FREEPOST
Southport
Merseyside
PR8 1BR
(01704) 542373
(Supplies back supports)

The Back Shop Ltd
24 New Cavendish Street
London
W1M 7LM
(0171) 935 9148 (Helpline)

British Acupuncture Association and Register
34 Alderney Street
London
SW1V 3EU
(0171) 834 1012/6229

British Chiropractic Association
29 Whitley Street
Reading
Berks
RG2 0EG
(01734) 757557

The Chartered Society of Physiotherapy
14 Bedford Row
London
WC1R 4ED
(0171) 242 1941

The Fellowship of Sports Masseurs and Therapists
BM Soigneur
London
WC1N 3XX

General Council and Register of Osteopaths
56 London Street
Reading
Berks
RG1 4SQ
(01734) 757557

National Ankylosing Spondylitis Society
5 Grosvenor Crescent
London
SW1X 7ER
(0171) 235 9585

National Back Pain Association
31/33 Park Road
Teddington
Middlesex
TW111 0AB
(0181) 977 5474

National Osteoporosis Society
PO Box 10
Radstock
Bath
Avon
BA3 3YB
(01761) 431594 (Helpline)

The Pain Society
9 Bedford Square
London
WC1B 3RA
(Send SAE for register of pain clinics)

Self-Help in Pain (SHIP)
33 Kingsdown Park
Tankerton
Kent
CT5 2DT
(01227) 264677

Scoliosis Association UK
2 Ivebury Court
325 Latimer Road
London
W1O 6RA
(0181)964 5343

ROBINSON FAMILY HEALTH

All your health questions answered in a way you really understand.

Titles available from booksellers or direct from Robinson include:

Arthritis: What *Really* Works
Dava Sobel & Arthur C. Klein
1–85487–290–7   £7.99

Asthma
Megan Gressor
1–85487–386–5   £2.99

Bad Backs: A Self-Help Guide
Leila Henderson
1–85487–388–1   £2.99

Bulimia Nervosa: A Guide to Recovery
Dr Peter Cooper
1–85487–171–4   £5.99

Headaches: Relief at Last
Megan Gressor
1–85487–391–1   £2.99

Let's Get Things Moving: Overcoming Constipation
Pauline Chiarelli and Sue Markwell
1–85487–389–X   £2.99

Massage for Common Ailments
Penny Rich
Illustrated in full colour
1–85487–315–6   £4.99

Menopause Made Easy
Kendra Sundquist
1–85487–383–0   £2.99

Pregnancy and Birth
Kerrie Lee
1–85487–390–3   £2.99

Overcoming IBS
Dr Christine P. Dancey & Susan Backhouse
1–85487–175–7   £5.99

Practical Aromatherapy
Penny Rich
Illustrated in full colour
1–85487–315–6   £4.99

The Recovery Book: A Self-Help Guide for Recovering Alcoholics, Addicts and Their Families
Al J. Mooney, Arlene Eisenberg & Howard Eisenberg
1–85487–292–3   £9.99

Women's Waterworks
Pauline Chiarelli
1–85487–382–2   £2.99

You *Can* Beat Period Pain
Liz Kelly
1–85487–381–4   £2.99

How to Order

To order a book, please send a cheque (made out to Robinson Publishing Ltd) or postal order to the address below, adding 50p per title for postage and packing. Send to: **Family Health, Robinson Publishing Ltd, 7 Kensington Church Court, London W8 4SP.**

While this information was correct at the time of going to press, details may change without notice.